Circle of Life
Pond Life

Written by David Stewart
Illustrated by Carolyn Scrace
Created and designed by David Salariya

W
FRANKLIN WATT
LONDON•SYDNEY

Contents

Introduction   6

Finding a mate   8

Courtship   11

Mating   12

The eggs hatch   15

Tadpoles   16

Dangerous times   19

From tadpoles to froglets   20

From froglets to frogs   23

Autumn arrives   24

Winter settles in   27

Pond life through the year   28

Words about pond life   30

Index   31

Introduction

Every pond is different. Many of the plants, insects and animals shown in this book may be found in ponds near you.

Frogs, newts, fish and some birds all live on or in ponds. In this book, you will see how they find mates, how their young are born and how the young grow into adults.

Fox

Magpie

Male frog

Finding a mate

In the spring all the creatures living in and around the pond begin to look for mates.

The male frog sits on a lily pad in the sun. Frogs spend most of their lives in or close to fresh water.

Male stickleback

Newt

Great pond snail

Male
duck

Courtship

The stickleback male does a zig-zag dance in the water to attract a female.

The male frog attracts a mate by making his throat swell. Then he croaks loudly. The female answers him in chirps and grunts.

Female newt

Newts live on land as well as in water. In spring, they enter the water to find a mate. Male and female newts dance before mating. This is called courtship.

Water louse

Duckweed

Mating

When the male frog has attracted a female they can mate. The female frog lays about 3,000 eggs. Then the male frog covers the eggs with sperm. This fertilises the eggs and they begin to grow.

The male stickleback builds a nest of dead leaves. He guards the nest to protect the female when she lays her eggs.

Female frog

Stickleback nest

Kingfisher

The eggs hatch

Dragonfly nymph

The fertilised frog's eggs stick together and sink to the bottom of the pond.

Frogspawn

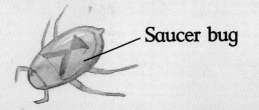

Saucer bug

Tadpole

The jelly around the eggs swells and forms frogspawn. A few days later tadpoles hatch from the eggs.

Pond worm

15

Tadpoles

Seven weeks after
hatching, the tadpoles
still live underwater.
They breathe through their
gills and eat tiny plants.

The tadpoles' back legs start to
grow. As they get bigger, tadpoles
eat small water animals like water
fleas and pond worms.

Water spider's air bubble

Pond worm

Dangerous times

Great diving
beetle

Two weeks later, the
tadpoles' gills disappear.
The tadpoles then start
to breathe using lungs.

Many creatures in the pond like
to eat tadpoles. Even insects
such as the great diving beetle
will catch and eat them.

Water scorpion

Tadpoles

Caddis fly

Pond skater

From tadpoles to froglets

As spring turns into summer the tadpoles become young frogs, called froglets. They can now swim to the surface of the pond and breathe air. Froglets have long sticky tongues, good for catching insects.

From froglets to frogs

White water lily

Frogs

Pike

Frogs are amphibians. This means they can live in and out of water. Above the surface of the pond, the fully grown frogs can be a good meal for a fox.

Pike are a danger to every small creature in the pond. They lie close to plants and catch their prey by surprise.

23

Autumn arrives

All the animals born in the spring are now adults. As summer changes to autumn the weather becomes cooler and wetter. Birds migrate to warmer places. Some animals prepare to hibernate.

Caddis fly
larva case

Winter settles in

Life in the pond is much quieter in winter. Many creatures and plants look dead, but they are not. They are saving their energy for when the warmer weather returns in the spring.

The frog has found a place to hibernate. He will sleep all through winter among the rotting leaves at the bottom of the pond.

Pond life through the year

In spring, the adult frogs look for mates.

Many of the pond animals go through courtship dances to attract a mate.

During mating, the female frog's eggs are fertilised by the male.

After 21 days tadpoles hatch from the frogspawn.

The tadpoles grow into froglets. Their gills disappear and the froglets breathe with lungs.

By the end of the summer, the froglets have become fully grown frogs. They will soon be looking for their own mates.

Words about pond life

Amphibians
Creatures able to live in water or on land. They begin their lives in water.

Courtship
The special things a male does to attract a female.

Fertilisation
When an egg and sperm join together. The egg and sperm will become a baby.

Froglet
A young frog.

Frogspawn
The sticky eggs of a frog that float on the surface of the water. Tadpoles hatch from frogspawn.

Gills
These are needed by animals to breathe underwater. They are on the outside of the body.

Hatch
When a baby creature comes out of its egg.

Hibernate
To sleep through the winter.

Larva
The form an insect takes after hatching from its egg.

Lungs
These are needed by creatures to breathe air. They are inside the body.

Mating
The joining of a male (father) to a female (mother) to make babies.

Migrate
When an animal travels a long way, at certain times of the year, to find a warmer or cooler place to live.

Nymph
A young dragonfly.

Prey
An animal that is killed by another for food.

Sperm
The liquid from the male that joins the egg from the female to produce a baby.

Tadpole
The small creature that hatches from a frog's egg.

Index

A
amphibians 23, 30
autumn 24

C
caddis fly 20, 24
courtship 11, 28, 30

D
dragonfly 9
dragonfly nymph 15, 30
duck 9, 11
duckling 17

E
eggs 12, 15, 28, 30

F
female 9, 11, 12, 28, 30
fertilisation 12, 15, 28,
  30
fox 8, 23
froglets 20, 21, 23, 29, 30
frogs 6, 8, 9, 11, 12, 13, 15,
  20, 23, 27, 28, 29, 30
frogspawn 15, 29, 30

G
gills 16, 17, 19, 29, 30

great diving beetle 19
great pond snail 8

H
hibernate 24, 27, 30

I
insects 6, 20, 30

K
kingfisher 15

L
larva 24, 30
leaves 12, 25, 27
lily pads 8, 23
lungs 19, 29, 30

M
magpie 8
males 8, 10, 11, 12, 28,
  30
mates 6, 8, 11, 28, 29, 30
mating 12, 28, 30
migration 24, 30
mosquitoes 9

N
nest 12

newts 6, 8, 10, 11, 17

P
pike 23
plants 6, 16, 23, 27
pond skater 20
pond worm 15, 16
prey 23, 30

S
saucer bug 15
sperm 12, 30
spring 6, 11, 20, 27, 28
sticklebacks 8, 9, 11, 12
summer 20, 24, 29

T
tadpoles 15, 16, 17, 19,
  20, 29, 30
tongues 20

W
water 8, 11, 23, 30
water flea 16, 17
water louse 11
water spider 14, 16
white water lily 23
winter 27, 30

Language Consultant: Betty Root
Natural History Consultant: Dr Gerald Legg

Editors: Karen Barker Smith
                           Stephanie Cole

Created, designed and produced by
The Salariya Book Company Ltd
Book House,
25 Marlborough Place,
Brighton BN1 1UB

Visit the Salariya Book Company at
www.salariya.com

A CIP catalogue record for this book is available
from the British Library.

ISBN 0 7496 4231 9

Published in Great Britain in 2002 by
Franklin Watts
96 Leonard Street,
London EC2A 4XD

Franklin Watts Australia
56 O'Riordan Street,
Alexandria, NSW 2015

Printed in China.